SPEAKING UP in Poetry & Prose

By Jack Joseph Prather

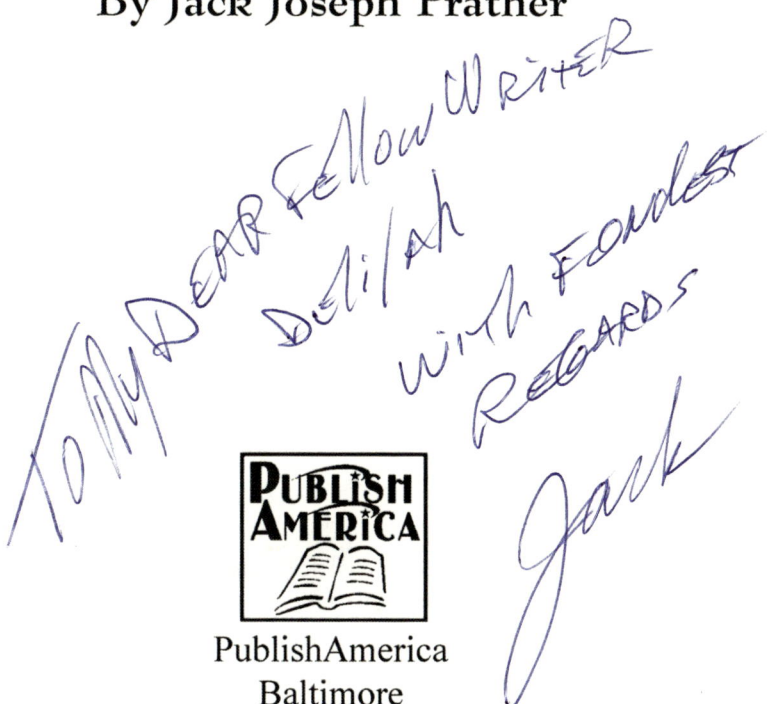

PublishAmerica
Baltimore

© 2007 by Jack Joseph Prather.
All rights reserved. No part of this book may be reproduced, stored in a retrieval system or transmitted in any form or by any means without the prior written permission of the publishers, except by a reviewer who may quote brief passages in a review to be printed in a newspaper, magazine or journal.

First printing

At the specific preference of the author, PublishAmerica allowed this work to remain exactly as the author intended, verbatim, without editorial input.

ISBN: 1-4241-0871-3
PUBLISHED BY PUBLISHAMERICA, LLLP
www.publishamerica.com
Baltimore

Printed in the United States of America

Mrs Jean Williams
14426 SE Auburn Blck Diamnd Rd
Auburn, WA 98092

Mrs Jean Williams
14426 SE Auburn Blck Diamnd Rd
Auburn, WA 98092

Acknowledgements

Gratitude for insightful evaluations, sharp editing and constant support go to Pam, my treasure, for her guidance as I forged this book from the depths of me. She redirected me when I got off message, warned me when I displayed hubris, and excels as my life and business partner.

Thanks to: Monk Larsen, a poet in his own right and a thoughtful intellectual for his critique and encouragement at the start of this project; to Dr. Don Emon for the spirited in-depth discussions that covered every issue imaginable; to congregants of the Unitarian-Universalist Fellowship of Hendersonville N.C. who share a love of diversity; to my writing mentors, especially the late editor of The New Jersey Herald Marlin Morgan who gave me column writing opportunity, challenge and free subject rein for 12 years; and to family members and friends who helped shape my view of the world for allowing me to witness their viewpoints without rancor.

Social and political inspiration began with John F. Kennedy, who moved me to enter politics as a consultant and understand that life is not fair but that we all must forge forward; Martin Luther King, who demonstrated that non-violence and fortitude are more than just virtues; Bill Gates, who recently dedicated a significant portion of his immense fortune to worthwhile causes; James Michener, who authored fact-based novels of intellectual integrity and extraordinary depth; and the many who give of themselves and their assets to the common good, wherever they are.

Introduction
SPEAKING UP in Poetry and Prose

By Jack Joseph Prather

Poetry and prose must speak honestly and be true to intent to give credibility to inner voices and philosophies, observations of nature and the cosmos, feelings of passion and compassion, compulsion to protest or dissent, desire to pay homage or criticize perceived societal wrongs: all primary themes reflected within this book.

SPEAKING UP in Poetry and Prose attempts to plant seeds or express points-of-view designed to evoke thought and exploration about deeper meaning about the subject matter. The author hopes it will lead to discussions about important issues, ideas and observations in any forum: family, classroom, between friends.

Great modern poets crafted messages more clearly than the old masters, at least for me. Many are so well known they are recognized by first name: Walt, Robert, Edgar, Maya, Sylvia, T.S., Langston, Carl, Emily: who is your favorite? I admire but do not emulate them, for this book reflects only my personal inner voice, my format, my style, be it traditional, non-traditional or experimental.

A thousand years separated the following two expressions of old poetry and prose from authors who lived and wrote a half a world apart but their words of simple elegance and profound beauty remain timeless:

Alone and Looking at the Mountain:

All the birds have flown up and gone.
A lonely cloud floats leisurely by. We
never tire of looking at each other,
only the mountain and I.
				Li Po, 701-762

* * * * *

No man was ever yet a great poet
without at the same time being a
profound philosopher, for poetry
is the blossom and the fragrance
of human thought, human passions,
emotions, language.
		Samuel Taylor Coleridge, 1772-1834

Poetry and Prose by Number

page

1. Speaking Up	citizen voices	11
2. View from the Cave	anti-war	12
3. Sandburg Homage	to the people's poet	13
4. Journey	religious maturity	14
5. The Bully Boys Club	bullying	16
6. Venting the Flames	flag-burning	17
7. Owls Have No Teeth	importance of learning	18
8. If in Doubt Leave Them Out	the Pledge of Allegiance	19
9. Haiku, Too	five pieces	20
10. The Last At-Bat	baseball is life	21
11. Clickety-Click	poignant obsession	23
12. Soldier's Lament	anti-Iraq war	24
13. The Butterfly	overcoming fear	25
14. Drops of Dew	African suffering	26
15. Small g	response to zealotry	27
16. Reality and Other Illusions	facing the facts	28
17. 26	communication	29
18. •	stem cell research	30
19. Connections	we are one	31
20. Immigrants Are Us	unless we are Indian	32
21. A Tragedy in Brooklyn	a sad memory	34
22. Questions of Choice	women's right to choose	36
23. Joey	searching	37
24. Treasures	childhood memories	38
25. Sticks and Stones	leaders' slurs	39
26. The Longest Moment	humanity	40
27. Lies, Fibs and Other Truths	skewing the truth	41
28. Recipe	what made me	42
29. Lacy and Connor	the Peterson Case	43
30. The Six Senses	'feeling' is the sixth	44
31. A Scarlet H	for hypocrisy	46
32. Power	use yours wisely	47

33. A Half-Truth	the Second Amendment	48
34. Cutting and Running	from truth	49
35. Dark	facing fear	50
36. Eminent Domain	taking your land	51
37. Green Irish Eyes	love	52
38. Taxes Are Good	waste is not	53
39. Heat	global warming	54
40. A Butterfly for Camryn	grandchildren	55
41. Kill	capitol punishment	56
42. Thing	about—ugh, can't say it	57
43. Run Deer Run	hunting	58
44. Staying Healthy	rising healthcare costs	59
45. Make a List	decision-making	60
46. White and Black	inter-racial adoption	61
46. The Conversation	with God	62
48. Two Worlds	the rich and not	64
49. Serendipity	ah, home	65
50. Itty Bitty Ditty	signoff	66

Back-Stories and Briefs   67
Back Stories and Briefs   69

1. Speaking Up

Search for answers and search for clues
   try to make sense from the nightly news
      but you should know if you dig too deep
         you might get the bends and little sleep.

But it is our obligation, if not then who's?
   to know our country's actions and views
      and to ponder each decision that is made
         then offer honest views and not be afraid.

We can all contribute to the greater good
   if we speak up when we know we should
      when we do not is when things go wrong
         maybe silence was our problem all along.

2. View from the Cave

You threw a stone then I threw two
   you aimed at me and I aimed at you
      we tossed them with vengeful thirst
         and it did not matter who threw first.

We learned stones were not enough
   so we made spears to make us tough
      as our weapons grew so did our hate
         an evil duo that could decide our fate.

Your tribe, mine, does anybody care
   about the reality in a doomsday scare
      but if we don't and it fulfills its mark
         we will all be doomed to eternal dark.

We must conquer this wartime dread
   before it finds us and renders us dead
      or banishes us to caves hurling stones
         and pondering all the unknown bones.

3. Sandburg Homage

The poet's words still echo, you can hear it in the breeze
immortal lessons that resonate in his water and his trees
his Connemara never slumbers in the winter or the night
stalwart guardian of his legacy, illuminated by his light.

The forest gave him refuge, the creatures gave him peace
the silence played the music he wished would never cease
the ideals he bravely wrote of gave new hope to everyone
who sought to find a better life before that life was done.

His philosophical insights framed by an historian's touch
memorialized Abe Lincoln for giving Americans so much
with courage and conviction both strived for brotherhood
to attain equality for all and to protect the common good.

Fame and fortune were thrust upon the poet of the people
and Connemara was his church, a mountain for a steeple
his beloved home is revered as a monument to his dignity
Carl Sandburg: poet, author and exemplar for humanity.

The Poet

The poet comes
with a giant mind.
He carefully crafts
poetic truths and ideals
for hearts and minds
and inspires us all.

4. Journey

Sliding on the marble floors of an empty church.
Hunkering in a pew to the eerie sound of silence.
Memorizing stained glass colors backlit by sun.
Wondering if I belong.
When I was 10.

Kissing a bishop's ring, confessing imagined sin.
Partaking of the bread and wine of communions.
Reciting psalms, prayers and pious meditations.
Hoping I belong.
When I was 12.

Carrying a cross leading the choir to altar pews.
Striding to soft organ music and elegant hymns.
Ringing a brass bell, holding a Bible for a priest.
Pretending I belong.
When I was 14.

Figuring out those things I do and do not believe.
Accepting those doubts I innately had always felt.
Realizing that what I don't believe is right for me.
Knowing I do not belong.
When I was 18.

Coping with believers who denigrate my journey.
Hoping to calmly debate those willing to be open.
Learning few want to hear another point of view.
Wondering where I belong.
When I was 20.

Learning the difference of possible and knowable.
Respecting any faith of others that is not injurious.
Continuing to seek truth knowing I cannot find it.
Finding I belong in the journey.
When I was a man.

5. The Bully Boys Club

Bully Boy Jake Pyle was the toughest man in town
he had wide shoulders and wore a fearsome frown
when the big man spoke it seemed more like a roar
and his glare caused many men to bolt for the door.

Jake saw what he wanted then he took what he saw
knowing for certain no one would dare call the law
they all knew what Jake could do when put to a test
he could scare off half the men then beat up the rest.

Jake ruled The Blue Ox Bar by using fear and fame
until Jim Tace walked in to call the big man's game
the newcomer smiled then put out his hand to shake
slyly aware no one could trust mean Bully Boy Jake.

Jake Pyle figured the score and tightly balled his fist
swung savagely at Jim Tace but he narrowly missed
Jim escaped the blow with a confident nimble grace
then smashed a Blue Ox stool into Bully Boy's face.

It was strange to see Jake lying prone upon the floor
being dragged by a new bully boy out the front door
then to see the victor return to claim a Blue Ox table
with intent to lend his name to the Bully Boys' fable.

Patrons pitied poor Jake with jaw and spirit broken
about this man no kind words would ever be spoken
Jim claimed the Ox as his turf to everybody's dread
until new Bully Boy Jake Pyle's son killed him dead.

6. Venting the Flames

The cloth flamed then dissolved to ash
    incinerated by a person crass and rash
        I was galled and appalled about the rat
            who burnt the flag that let him do that.

In what nation would he prefer to live?
    What contribution has he here to give?
        Is he full of hate or acting on a whim?
            Is he blind to the nation that bred him?

The Constitution—The Bill of Rights
    allow those awful flag-burning sights
        protect any protester obeying the law
            even the misguided flag-burner I saw.

Our liberty was earned under that flag
    it was painful to see it burned like a rag
        the tear in my eye was my solemn reply
            as wind vented Old Glory up to the sky.

7. Owls Have No Teeth

I've discovered about most things I really have no clue
so I attempt to remember every little factoid, don't you?
All the strange things new I learn that I know to be true
I just add to my trivia list for they don't affect my view.

I'm sorry to say I hate the way that often during a chat
a young person will declare: I don't need to know that!
for they will regret someday they stood so mentally pat
when they do not have a clue and it is their brain at bat.

They question the importance of all that mundane stuff
and the value of trivia when they already know enough
they say it cannot be of help when life gets really rough
to answer them is very important but is also very tough.

If you absorb more facts perhaps your brain will grow
and maybe you will know quiz answers on a TV show.
You will always flourish from greater knowledge flow
with pride in yourself when it is you that's in the know.

Many of those trivial things I learned I often call upon,
I'll pick a few for you to review others are simply gone,
some are funny, some are droll, some may turn you on,
if you ponder each new fact ideas could be their spawn.

Many reject the assertion that we evolved out of the sea
but mainstream scientists agree it produced you and me.
There are no Alien UFO's visiting from the stars we see,
they are a thousand lifetimes away and thus it cannot be.

A dromedary has only one hump and a camel boasts two.
A whale is a marine mammal out of the sea just like you.
Owls have no teeth but please do not ask how they chew,
but maybe those wise old owls know how we humans do.

8. If in Doubt Leave Them Out

Ike suggested two new words for our pledge in 19 and 54
   and said that if we would just pray to God almighty more
      America would become much better deep within its core,
         that a Pledge of Allegiance to Him is a duty not a chore.

Those simple words Under God were added to our creed
   citizens then were too timid to call this an intolerant deed
      but more than a half-century later some now loudly plead
         a return to the original version that fulfills a greater need.

Religious politics paved the way for the words to be put in
   the same politics continue to stifle the ever-increasing din
      from voices of America that believe forcing prayer is sin
         that a misguided majority produced an undemocratic win.

It is often slow and painful to overcome a majority's clout
   but we must try to attain democracy, it's what it's all about
      until those words are removed, this solution I silently shout
         go ahead and recite your pledge, if in doubt leave them out!

9. Haiku, Too

Do you feel haiku?
Winter mind slowly matures
to reap what spring sowed.
        * * * *

Little visitor bird
hovering on blurred wings.
The world too needs peace.
        * * * *

Roiling river, mud bank,
legacies of chemistry.
Still, butterflies fly.
        * * * *

Creaks and groans and stones,
the Majors seem beyond reach.
The seasons wind down.
        * * * *

Deafening silence
penetrates the forest tree
and seals the closed mind.

10. The Last At-Bat

The kaleidoscope refracts the game of life in a geometric prism.
I peek within and still can see—

A child's leather glove that glistens and smells of Neat's Foot Oil
and clasps a tattered baseball in a pocket tightly bound
with cord for safe storage underneath a pillow.

Vivid visions from home plate of the curve of the earth in deepest
center field, the architectural symmetry reflected by a
field of green grass and smoothed infield dirt.

Memories of pitchers towering above mountain mounds throwing
curve balls that 'fall off the table' and 90-mph fastballs
that allow one-third of a second to hit-the-deck.

The exhilaration from the crack of a bat, an extra-base blow, a relay
out, a slump-ending base hit, an extra-inning victory,
a great catch and a badge-of-courage 'raspberry'.

Lessons about how to execute a sac-bunt, shorten up to keep a ball
in play, work a pitcher for a walk, take one for the team
and know like Yogi "It ain't over 'til it's over".

The pride of championships, double-header sweeps, walk-off hits,
cheers, umps bellowing "Yer safe!" and coping with K's,
painful errors, razzing and critical coaches.

My game of life kaleidoscope contains statistics, wins, losses, but
more importantly captures the special magic of a father
bonding with his son at a baseball game.

I live in that kaleidoscope where I see me playing one more game, but it is the bottom of the ninth and my last at-bat, so I better bear down if I want to stay alive.

11. Clickety-Click

Clickety-click, clickety-click, the train hurtles through the night
warning all those within its path with headlights beaming bright
and its whistle blares in the evening air a mournful ghostly song
it won't slow down through any town for its journey is too long.

The cadence of those clickety-clicks provides a calming charm
as I catch sight of a bedroom light gone dim on a passing farm
and wonder if anyone who lives within the fleeting houses I see
could catch a glimpse and wonder about any passer-by like me.

As daybreak dawns and my journey ends I know it is time to go
but I will always wonder about the folks that I can never know
and I am sad to say that on that day I uttered a sorrowful sigh
for I may have lost a lover or friend because I passed them by.

Clickety-click, clickety-click is a symphony that still plays inside
and I see each night when I flick off the light visions of that ride
through it all I know it must stop and if not I should admit defeat
that I must abandon wistful dreams and bond with people I meet.

Yet whirling wheels on tracks of steel still echo through my nights
I seem fated to be forever possessed by mythical melancholy sights
they haunt me and taunt me deep within but I must move on I know
for I got on the train that lives in my brain more than 20 years ago.

12. Soldier's Lament

It was only a moment, it seemed like more
on a fateful morning on that foreign shore
as I aimed my rifle and my heart beat fast
and I killed a man but he was not the last.

My enemy would have slain me if he could
if he had fired first as he thought he would
I saw life ebb away from his piercing eyes
with not one murmur and no parting cries.

I remember him lying there so deathly still
and wonder who cries because of that kill
is it a family like mine that he left behind?
forever torn by war so unholy and unkind.

I continued that mission again and again
I became inured to wartime fruits of pain
battling on for those comrades who died
their fates determined by those who lied.

I will stalwartly fight any foreign threat
to safeguard my family and America, yet
I must now lament the American invasion
that pre-empted the power of persuasion.
(Please see Back-Story)

13. The Butterfly

A little caterpillar creeps close to the ground
seeking any place where peace can be found
she peeks left, then right, then straight ahead
too afraid to stop, she inches onward instead.

The tiny green insect, so beautiful and bright
searches deeply within to summon her might
to learn from mistakes through trial and error
and battle with strength the turmoil and terror.

Those little caterpillar legs can't run very fast
but they keep on churning, determined to last
they'll remain in the race and stay on the trail
and help outrun the doubters certain she'd fail.

Little butterfly discards her green furry coat
flutters fragile wings and soon begins to float
the first majestic flight carries her into the sky
with new gossamer wings that allow her to fly.

She can escape the earth with each new flight
can just flap those wings and soar out of sight
time is her mentor for she is still quite young
with many a day left for her songs to be sung.

May the sun shine brightly wherever she goes
may the calm water buoy her wherever it flows
the cocoon kept her safe, the wings set her free
to create more caterpillars for everyone to see.

14. Drops of Dew

Bones protrude within gossamer skin
taut black casings ready to yield
to the relentless sun.

Beautiful blue sky with white clouds
are but deceptions to the natives
of this arid feral land.

Parched mouth silent to the outrages
a frail mother protects her child
and her quiet dignity.

Husband and father both surrendered
long ago to cruel natural forces
of land without mercy.

Pain numbed by countless atrocities
she silently considers their fate
and aliens with gifts.

Maternal fear of sole survival arises
as Samaritans try to rescue her
and their consciences.

They are but drops of dew in a fire
soon to return home to express
regrets and concerns.

Ever to be haunted by hollow eyes
silent cries and gossamer skin
of a mother no more.

15. Small g

Any god who condemns me to an everlasting flame
and his followers who perpetuate this tragic shame
who judge me unkindly because I am not the same
will be found guilty of hate in life's court of blame.

god is in the heart of man, in animals roaming free
in the majesty of a mountain, in the beauty of a tree
in the smell of dewy grass, in rainbows that we see
in brotherly love that should flow from you and me.

I do not need a vengeful deity to tell me what to do
I do not abide condemnation from him or from you
that I live as a respectful and moralistic man is true
I will demand if I cannot command respect I am due.

If your all-powerful god controls everything we are
explain to me why he allows such evil, hate and war
why his cruelly martyred son is what we waited for
when love lessons could have graced us to the core.

Explain to me a holocaust, 911 and the end of days
without invoking myths about 'his mysterious ways'
why in messianic murdering hordes everyone prays
to god when killing others in his name earns praise.

My gay and lesbian friends wonder—I wonder too
would love end at the church door if they were you
if you would end the science with promise to renew
the temple of an ailing body if that temple held you.

Live your wrath and sentence me to hell if you must
ignore my effort to live a life of caring sharing trust
but be careful of your judgment when we turn to dust
a vengeful god would doom you too if he is truly just.

16. Reality and Other Illusions

What is reality and what is untrue?
   what are humans supposed to do?
      what are the reasons we are here?
         is facing death something to fear?

What is 'is', that is all we can know
   we unveil new purpose as we grow
      that we are alive is reason to crow
         end of life is just part of that flow.

Meaning of reality born from a view
   leads to illusions that often go askew
      facts matter for they are what's true
         they combine to show us what to do.

Faith is plentiful for most have belief
   but when misused it can lead to grief
      a seller of hate is worse than a thief
         a truth teller has justice in his brief.

17. 26

Consonants number 20
but sometimes 21
only y changes definition
hard to know just when.

Vowels number five
but can grow to 6
they often make mischief
with alphabetical tricks.

Not much to work with
26 letters in all
and it's very hard to judge
where each should fall.

When you wax poetic
get the letters right
because if you do not
you'll be waxing all night.

There are no shortcuts
but do not be shy
only 26 to choose from
you can do it if you're sly.

18. •

I am Stem Cell no bigger than a dot
I can not think or feel
but in medical research I mean a lot.

I can help cure many dread diseases
but first as you know
I must convert those this displeases.

Parkinson's, Alzheimer's I can cure
spinal cord injury too
if Americans affirm my way is pure.

Our president cut stem cell research
said it was 'the word'
spoken by his god within his church.

No one would be helped right away
our First-Lady stated
so we must forget it and simply pray.

It is so ironic that now religious zeal
leads the fight against
scientific research designed to heal.

Jesus used miracles and noble deeds
the Holy Bible says
to help improve sick people's needs.

If anybody asks "Who can help me?"
my answer is clear:
"It is I, Stem Cell, a cure soon to be!"

19. Connections

Every thing seems connected to every
other thing in the universe, each person
somehow bound to each other person.

> A rainbow to a sky, a meaning to a hi
> a heart to a man, a mother to a clan.

The chaos of evolution gave precious
and wondrous gifts of man and animal
to populate and nurture the earth.

> A core to a peach, a grain to a beach
> a hope to a care, a wish to a prayer.

Micro-dot earth shares gravity with a
6-million-mile-long, 83 million degree
gas comet racing at 1.6 million-mph.

> A second to a year, a sorrow to a tear
> a branch to a tree, a droplet to a sea.

What has gone before can't be undone
but in it are lessons of what may come
the main one is, we must act as one.

> A soldier to a corps, a battle to a war
> a start to a cease, a stop to a peace.

20. Immigrants Are Us

Before you get ultra excited
and your snarl becomes a bite
at all those immigrants who you
don't know just remember that your
papa and your mama came from theirs
who came from theirs so you better keep
your own counsel until you first determine
from whence they all came or you just might
be sniping at yourself. Wouldn't that be a kick?

Human nature seems to trick
us into believing we own entire
nations, states, towns and blocks
when all we really own is what we
paid for to live in and on while others
seek only to dream and then scratch and
claw mostly peacefully and legally to make
it come true however and whenever they can.
Should we help legalize those who want to stay?

Many Americans in America
after they exit a city for a quaint
town sing out Katie Bar the Door
to dissuade invaders who will cause
traffic to increase and higher taxes and
the same negative impacts as they brought
when they invaded the town and irked natives
who want things to be stay the way they are and
used to be. This is a familiar position everywhere.

We are all immigrants from
some other place either foreign

or domestic and should be warm
and welcoming of other immigrants
if we are to remain the melting pot first
envisioned by our forefathers with hopes
we would become a symbol of inclusion for
world citizens seeking safe refuge in the USA.
We should embrace them for immigrants are us!

21. A Tragedy in Brooklyn

Breathing high Brooklyn air
in the safe place of my
rooftop four stories
above 40th Street.

Above the woman who had
waved to me a minute
ago, a lifetime ago,
now suddenly still.

My private sanctuary visited
so many times before
shattered, no longer
hallowed or mine.

I lean on a jagged concrete
ledge, squint through
fire escape openings
to the panic below.

Sirens scream their way to
Georgie's mother, dead
because her window
sill disintegrated.

She was cleaning windows
now honks clear a way
for the ambulance
to claim her.

People below sob and wail.
An icy wind whistles
and haunts me as I
shiver silently.

I stare at the darkening sky.
Stars blink weakly and
birds fly to safety
in the horizon.

My mother calls to me from
our window just below.
It's time for dinner
and sympathy.

22. Questions of Choice

Do poignant choices, life or death,
haunt the unready unsteady
conscience, bewilder
the unprepared?

Do the judging voices that shout
'Shame, you have no right
to kill the soul within'
offer solutions?

Why do their selective concerns
not include unjust war, the
death penalty, genocide,
the hungry poor?

Why are their eyes and minds
shut to the whys of choice,
and why do they not
see other views?

Should not choice of abortion
for convenience or for
birth control first be
squarely faced?

Would not abortion be healing
for rape victims, incest,
those in poor health or
extreme duress?

Should not choice be the right
of those who carry the
fetus then must deal
with their choice?

23. Joey

Joey found a coin along the shore
when just a teen-aged boy
now he hunts all day to find more
with his metal-detector toy.

He'll locate baubles buried deep
much better if he does not
for he even hunts within his sleep
because that is all he's got.

Joey never sees the ocean's sheen
does not taste its salty air
or hear its waves of rolling green
or enjoy its calming care.

Again today although he planned
to continue his daily grind
he'll be buried beneath the sand
all his treasures left behind.

24. Treasures

I never had much money but I never felt poor
for when I was a kid I found treasures galore
in Sunset Park, down at the harbor and more
as I roamed streets new treats were in store.

Dodgers in blue made every day seem bright
Greenwood Cemetery became eerie at night
the Statue of Liberty reigned within my sight
seeing her seemed to make everything right.

I would sneak on a subway Manhattan bound
and play for a day in the magical city I found
where skyscrapers, shops and hoboes abound
when in the Big Apple I'd just ramble around.

I'd peek in the library and gawk at Broadway
stop in Saint Patrick's and watch people pray
tour through Central Park for half of the day
until the ominous darkness curtailed my stay.

There was lots of free stuff and all of it good
I'd walk many blocks to see a strange 'hood
I savored it then and would return if I could
to stand again where that young kid stood.

25. Sticks and Stones

I did not know until I was told
in their public comment mean and bold
that if I opposed the Iraq war
I was just like Nazi sympathizers before.

That didn't end the evil slander
they continued to lie, continued to pander
stating with a fearsome dread
that I may be a fascist communistic red!

I did not realize until they said
my view would cause more American dead
and that it was unpatriotic, too
to disagree with the great decider's crew.

American history that I know
teaches this is dishonest and just not so
I stand proudly to offer dissent
and bow to no man's dishonorable bent.

I try to talk with calm and tact
and influence others with logic and fact
I know what they said is untrue
so the only response I will make is: boo!

26. The Longest Moment

The courtroom was so jammed it created a din
   then hushed when the judge and jury strode in
      our verdict is unanimous a sad foreman said
         murder in the first-degree he somberly read.

She sobbed and wailed and shook and flailed
   was dutifully handcuffed led away and jailed
      the murderess now worried if her ultimate fate
         would be a life in prison or death by the state.

Reporters gathered to make predictions galore
   about what penalty Alice Anderson had in store
      they were cynical and merciless and cold as ice
         for no matter her sentence it would not be nice.

But their humanity revived as the foreman arose
   to render the final decision that 12 jurors chose
      "Have you reached a verdict?" was asked next
         "We have" said the juror who read from a text.

The split second before their decision was read
   was the longest moment, it filled us with dread
      would Alice live or die we were about to learn
         either sentenced to prison or doomed to burn.

The spectators were filled with a sense of gloom
   until the words life in prison echoed in the room
      she should not die the dozen jurors had agreed
         deciding that she would live but never be freed.

But the epilogue that followed was tragic to see
   for Alice served only 12 years then was set free
      it didn't seem right and for a family it was hard
         paroling that woman who killed Charles Attard.

27. Lies, Fibs and Other Truths

Arlen said it was a magic bullet that day
    that helped kill American president JFK
        but skeptics like me continue to cry nay
            Spector's specter is just a story we say.

The jury stayed blind to the video show
    of Rodney being struck blow after blow
        the policemen said he was a furious foe
            but he did not resist, that much we know.

We invaded Iraq but for what is not clear
    they said Iraqis would rise up and cheer
        but an opposite response is what we hear
            instead of a peace there is now only fear.

Truth is truth and cannot flow from a need
    of political persuasion or matters of greed
        is the same for any race or color or creed
            and skewing it to suit is delusion in deed.

Fibs that are spoken to avoid hurt or pain
    are kind if they include no personal gain
        but a lie that skews truth is a sad refrain
            a supreme deceit that can lead to a stain.

28. Recipe

They provided the ingredients to make me
    a mind, such as it is, and that body you see
        mixed me and baked me with parental glee
            and often times seasoned and kneaded me.

Each daily grind and each roasting I faced
    enhanced my flavor and bettered my taste
        when I was sassy or my haste made waste
            the recipe was altered to help me be chaste.

They made a meal they hoped was gourmet
    instead their dish turned out more like puree
        maybe if it improves with age they will say
            we savor our efforts for he turned out okay.

29. Lacy and Connor

Staring moth-like at a flickering TV.
Pre-conceiving judgment from cruel,
mounting, electric, irresistible facts.
I bray aloud too early: "Scott did it!"
I hope he didn't, couldn't, wouldn't.

Pesky gnats of facts circle the light
to let murder out of its murky cave
for all to see. Too many the victims
we did not know, too brutal the acts
of this purveyor of death times two.

A sense of loss snares us in its web
of grief, of change, of pity for Lacy
and for Connor and for the family
and for those who believe in Scott.
On execution day, maybe for him.

30. The Six Senses

I see your sensuous beauty and
        rainbows on meadows
        clouds against blue sky
        stained glass in sunlight
        ocean waves raging
        forest trees towering

I hear your dulcet sounds and
        kittens purring
        church bells ringing
        rain peppering rooftops
        wind whistling
        sweet music playing

I smell your familiar scent and
        spring flowers
        fresh mown grass
        cookies in the oven
        new car leather
        steaks on the grill

I touch your sensual body and
        cold lake water
        rough tree bark
        marble floors
        baby cheeks
        ice-caked windows

I taste your happy tears and
            chocolate ice cream
            frosted mugs of beer
            gourmet creations
            movie popcorn
            ocean saltwater

I feel your abiding love and
            nature's wisdom
            order in the cosmos
            palpable memories
            friendship's warmth
            serendipity shared.

31. A Scarlet H

His daughter is a lesbian so he keeps silent
unwilling to offend his own
but was Dick like all his right wing friends
before her sexuality was known?

The president was felled by dread disease
research someday may cure
would Nancy really have supported it then
before that prognosis was sure?

Tom took his father off a life-saving device
said it was a right thing to do
then used his power to try to ban it forever
didn't he know it's our right too?

Rush called druggies profane and obscene
and did until he was found out
then said popping pills was okay with him
isn't that what he's really about?

Neo-cons bravely send our children to war
knowing their own seldom go
why do they remain on a discredited course
and not listen to those in the know.

I don't understand fully so I better not say
the reasons we are in this plight
are all those politicos who decide our fate
so totally blinded by the right?

I wonder if poet Hawthorne still was alive
would each get a scarlet letter
then wear on their forehead an H not an A
for hypocrisy is not any better!

32. Power

Kings inherit it, generals earn it
        power over their domains
        to lead nations or armies
        until that power wanes.

Absolute power, there's the rub
        it can lead into unjust war
        and rob us of our riches
        until we say no more.

Bosses have it, managers have it
        they use it when they must
        whenever they misuse it
        they sacrifice the trust.

If you earned your base of power
        please use it as you should
        ensuring that each cause
        is for a common good.

Power can be deserved or claimed
        by exerting will or strength
        but must be used properly
        to exist for any length.

33. A Half-Truth

Re-read the Second Amendment to the Constitution
the entire text, not just the select portion that
fits into your personal agenda.
Go ahead, it's only fair.

"The right of the people to keep and bear arms shall
not be infringed," is often quoted by the NRA
and its gun-owner members.
It is their right to say it.

But the amendment begins: "A well-regulated militia,
being necessary to the security of a free state"
a key qualifier they omit.
It is my right to say that.

I defend the right to keep and bear 'registered' guns
by educated citizen owners but am puzzled why
they resist this precaution.
Is my statement not fair?
This is not a slippery slope, conspiracy to confiscate
or track arms, or the denial of anyone's right
just a plea for fair debate.
One rule: an open mind.

First consider the truth, the whole truth and nothing
but the truth, not a half-truth and re consider
registration and training.
It could save many lives.

34. Cutting and Running

Does pure blind faith explain your faith in those who lied?
    who duped us in an unjust war where many thousands died?
        who never served yet claim sole ownership of patriotic pride?
            who send soldiers into harm's way while snugly safe stateside?

Explain your reason for this war with nary a plan to leave
    why you won't accept clear evidence of intention to deceive
        why a pre-emptive war is morally right to those who believe
            in only those who flout their faith then wear it on their sleeve.

I will support our troops no matter what and I always will
    I reject that I would cut and run as ignorant arrogant swill
        it is those who cut and run from truth that multiply the kill
            how many more must die in Iraq before they have their fill?

War is surely just when no other way can combat an enemy
    when the battlefield is a last resort but a necessary remedy
        yet sad that brave soldiers must die in any war's calamity
            but sometimes we must unite and fight to keep our liberty.

35. Dark

It was dark and cold and she heard rain
   pelting rhythmically on her window pane
      she burrowed beneath bed covers to hide
         and be warmly safe from terrors outside.

She bravely emerged to face a new day
   in light she'd be secure at work or play
      but as the illumination faded into night
         the darkness returned and with it fright.

Threats from an unseen and eerie force
   took over in the dark and set her course
      but finally she learned that what is best
         is to face fear and the hell with the rest.

Easy to be brave when you are unafraid
   difficult when an unseen threat is made
      but she challenged it and faced her fear
         and can now be proud for peace is near.

36. Eminent Domain

The Indian warrior silently defied his pain
    as torrents of rain swept across the plain
        and lightning danced with fading light
            to illuminate the atrocity in his sight.

Blue Cloud lived in peace most of his life
    in a forest village with Red Doe his wife
        until others came with treaties and war
            and he could not be as he was before.

'This is our land' the Indian long ago said
    but now all his warriors were lying dead
        the war was done and his tribe had lost
            his nation vanquished at terrible cost.

The invaders took the Indian lands for free
    and divided the spoils for you and for me
        the legacy of this we should now know
            is our land can become the next to go.

37. Green Irish Eyes

The embers flare then the embers die
   yet flare again when you are nearby
      your bright eyes flash in Irish green
         the prettiest eyes I have ever seen.

I first saw those eyes many years ago
   where did all those happy times go?
      never mind, we're still going strong
         twice again would not be too long.

Nothing has cooled and it never will
   you are my life and I adore you still
      I will be content if I can always see
         your green Irish eyes smiling at me.

38. Taxes Are Good

Complain about your taxes, when they go up frown
   but how would we live if the military shut down?
      moan about tax assessments, if they rise grouse
         but who would fix roads that go to your house?

No one likes the word tax for it seems like a curse
   but anger about a word makes everything worse
      the demon we know that must always be chased
         is a devil that haunts us: governmental waste!

Taxes enhance education and finance health care
   provide equal standards for workers everywhere
      safeguard Americans, secure planes and trains
         taxes are good if we control them with brains!

39. Heat

Most scientists and environmentalists cheer
    a conclusion that you may not want to hear
        that global warming is a threat to all
            and could result in earth's downfall!

If you pay scant attention to clear evidence
    or a scientific theory that makes good sense
        then your agenda is a dangerous view
            that heeds not what warming will do.

Icecaps are melting and ocean waters rising
    ozone is depleting and air quality demising
        they aren't yet a threat to you or me
            only to the future generations to be.

Who do you choose, your kids or yourself?
    why do you put good science on the shelf?
        we can slow warming if we act now
            to save our planet for we know how.

The world needs a plan of scientific scope,
    every nation contributing money and hope,
        everyone investing in the future good
            to save planet earth's neighborhood!

40. A Butterfly for Camryn

This paper butterfly is for Camryn, so little and so pure
   given with a love from Pop which will always be sure
      she can hang it in her room from a window or a door
         close tight her blue eyes at night then watch it soar.

It can't fly to the moon or star, they are much too high
   but it can float to a rooftop or tree that stands nearby
      she will be able to find it when she awakens each day
         catch it in her butterfly net then command it to stay.

Everyone loves grandkids, be they boys or be they girls
   enjoys their silly antics and those never-ending whirls
      twisting you around their finger is their special knack
         I just love to play with them and then give them back!

41. Kill

When her scale
tilts for the kill
justice is blind
to no pity find.

String him up
turn on the gas
flip that switch
see him twitch.

Just make sure
he's very dead
body and soul
put in a hole.

If we later find
he didn't do it
sorry we'll say
we had no dna.

Could it satisfy
all that he hurt
if he served life
in solitary strife?

Is death closure
for all involved
a reckoning day
no more to say?

If justice errors
produce the kill
how do we face
the human race?

42. Thing

I hate hate, pejoratives, meanness and guile
and when I'm attacked I prefer to just smile
but sometimes a high ground sinks to a low
this is that time for me, my heart tells me so.

I can not speak her name, it has a nasty ring
so from here on I will just label her 'Thing'
before this is over you will know who I mean
for she ousted Leona as the Queen of Mean.

When she compared herself to Mark Twain
I fell off a chair then checked with my brain
Clemens gibed hypocrites with ironic humor
'Thing' calls on acerbic and hateful rumor.

I won't give a life to her abominable quotes
and I do not doubt she'd get right-wing votes
Thing's maliciousness riled me into this stew
that devil who wears a black dress, not blue.

That she snorts and huffs are two more clues
and she is the bleached darling of Fox News
now to each reader the final questions I ask:
did you identify her, have I fulfilled my task?

43. Run Deer Run

Guiltless targets
at death's door
as pellets roar and arrows soar.

Unaware victims
of a fatal blow
deer playing in an open meadow.

Offering venison,
an elegant rack
for hidden pursuers to take back.

If hunters devour
game they kill
I respect them and I always will.

But if their hunt
is just for sport
they will never gain my support.

They do not care
this much I know
hunting tradition makes this so

But I truly believe
it should be said
a rack belongs on a deer head.

So run deer run,
nimble and fast
past an arrow or shotgun blast.

44. Staying Healthy

The poor working stiff will do the best he is able
to fill the tank with gas and put food on the table
forget about the extras or those promises to care
his life is getting costlier and that just isn't fair.

The harder he tries it seems the behinder he gets
while many others prosper he has no safety nets
his hope for a better future has been put on hold
and rising prices make him feel he's been rolled.

Who gets the benefits of our great medical care?
not the low-income family facing a health scare
much money is taken from obscene profit scams
by the fat cat executives who don't give a damn.

The working poor heard our leaders were friends
who would hard for them to reverse costly trends
but it didn't happen that way for they cut and ran
to instead give the fortunate every break they can!

45. Make a List

To have merit debate must be based on fact
    supported by evidence delivered with tact
        a method to help the closed mind retract
            a false conclusion and the truth to attract.

The view in a prism that an agenda makes
    distorts what we see, its answers are fakes
        sunlight is necessary, that's what it takes
            to have clear vision for all of our sakes.

Both sides too often are given equal weight
    even when their differences are very great
        eloquent discussion is an honorable trait
            but not an angry one that leads to hate.

Make a fair list of all the facts you can find
    rate the pros and cons even if it is a grind
        then ponder each one with an open mind
            and if you prevail, remember to be kind.

46. White and Black

They said
> it will not, can not work,
> white and black together,
> stick to your own race!

You said
> we will take 'any' child
> regardless of heritages
> for race does not matter.

You chose
> Craig, Keith and Debbie
> Todd, Adam and Jennifer
> to enter your trove of love.

You produced
> six university graduates
> productive honest adults
> half black and half white.

You received
> love, gratitude, respect
> healthy grandchildren.
> Mission accomplished!
> Rest in peace, Bob and Jesse.

46. The Conversation

Hello, Rachel, my daughter.
        My God, it's God!

Relax my dear, I have chosen to speak with you today.
I heard your prayer. How can I help you?
        Uh, Amy and I wish to get married.

Uh-huh.
        They won't let us. They say we're evil.

Excuuuse me! Who won't let you? Who is judging you?
        We got Bushwhacked.

Oh, him again. I might have to smite him for masquerading as me. Just answer these questions and
I will be your judge.
        I'll try.

Are you in love? How long have you been together?
Have you been faithful to each other? Are you each committed to the other?
        Yes, 15 years, yes and yes.

Who will your marriage hurt?
        No one.

Who will your marriage help?
        Us.

I see by your dossiers that both you and Amy live good
and decent lives and help others. You have the blessing
of your God.

Thank you from the bottom of our hearts, sir.

Make that thank you Ma'am.
Oops, sorry Ma'am. I didn't know.

God bless. I pronounce you wife and wife. Bye-bye, I'm late for a spiritual visit with Harry and Bob, and I gotta' find this Prather guy and ask him if this is what he calls poetry. Boy, I mean girl, does he need my help!
Thanks, God

48. Two Worlds

Bonus millions,
mega salaries,
perks galore.
We executives surely earned all this dough!

Expensive trips,
country clubs
much more.
That is why we must keep your wages low!

All the benefits,
annual raises,
up the score.
If a worker does not like it then he can go!

Market tipsters,
insider trading,
deals offshore.
All this is okay if it increases our portfolio!

Smart lawyers,
hidden tracks,
write our lore.
And we will keep the lion's share we know!

49. Serendipity

We carved a wooden sign, hung it on a tree
now everyone sees our home is 'Serendipity'
it sounds quite nice, its meaning is profound
you can feel the serenity if you look around.

Some days it feels like magic, others destiny
to live with so much joy in so much harmony
we never get blasé and never doubt our luck
it came from good fortune paired with pluck.

If we had a setback or a game was surely lost
we backed each other up, paid whatever cost
dusted ourselves off and began to fight again
and the sign on our tree kept us from the rain.

50. Itty Bitty Ditty

This might be my final poetry writing that you'll see

        then again it might not be

        so please stifle your glee

for while I'm still on the green side, not underneath

the more poems and prose I'll continue to bequeath.

That we don't always get what we hope for seems true

        if you hate this here's a cue

        toss it out and look for new

that would not break my heart and I promise not to cry

I know this itty ditty bitty bye-bye will just evoke a sigh

(Warning: a mystery novel may be my next try!)

Back-Stories and Briefs

These back-stories and briefs are offered to help provide perspective for the message poetry and prose in this book, although each piece must stand on its own; each is a microcosm that must live alone.

Where I write of the minority experience in America, or of a soldier who must kill in battle for his country, it is not from first-hand experience: I am speculating. But that speculation is born from a lifetime of attempting to understand how it would feel to actually live in the skin of a black person in America, and how it would affect me to kill another human being in war. I will never fully get there but am closer to understanding than those who do not try.

The material contains declaratives, philosophies, offers suggestions and ideas, and perhaps most importantly asks questions. My hope is that the direct or implicit questions will be pondered or discussed until answers evolve that are the closest possible to truth, not what one hopes or wishes to be truth. What is done with an answer remains an individual's choice.

I believe that what 'is' is! regardless of outside (or inside) influences. Truth cannot and should not be perceived and then believed primarily to fit a particular agenda, no matter how noble or desirable, especially in the face of seemingly incontrovertible fact or evidence.

Agreement with or confirmation of my points-of view is not necessarily my goal, although that would be fulfilling. What I do hope for a fair hearing. If my machinations include insights I will have succeeded in my primary mission.

Some influences on my perspectives are apparent through the quotes selected from speeches and writings by several notable

Americans, including an Indian chief, the premier civil rights leader of our time, a Supreme Court justice speaking for the majority, and the inscription on the welcoming tablet within the pedestal of the Statue of Liberty.

The back-stories and briefs are also born from the frustration and pain of college days in English Lit class trying to analyze and interpret poetry. It seemed the professor and many (of the more intellectual) students found different meanings in the same words and phrases, and then debated with varying degrees of enthusiasm to defend the validity of their conclusions. These were great mental and philosophical exercises and more power to them! But I must confess I was largely confused by obtuse and archaic words or phrases (my shortcoming) then and to some degree today.

Some of the pieces are metaphorical, some subtle to camouflage deeper meaning, some simply 'in your face'. All is intended to promote thought and discussion. None is intended to lecture or offend but no doubt will. C'est la vie.

A friend asked how long it took me to complete the collection and the answer is twofold: a few months and a lifetime. The contents reflect my views of the world, clarified as I pondered each issue, subject or idea. I attempted to focus on what is relevant to American thought and action in the 21st century, and then plumbed internally to find the most appropriate vehicle of expression (for me).

If the social or ethical positions or implied points-of-view positively influence yours or cause you to delve more deeply, then good for me!

Perspective: for 28 years I served as an independent political adviser and campaign consultant for several county democrats, two republican state legislators and two republican United States Congressmen. That said, I have made an effort to first construct and then share my views in a non-partisan fashion. My philosophy matches that of the Unitarian-Universalist Fellowship that embraces and respects everyone regardless of creed, race or color, or sexual orientation or preference, religious or not, gay or lesbian, or transgender. Everyone is welcome at UU and in my heart.

Back Stories and Briefs

1: Speaking Up
This poem is what this book is all about! For 13 years I had the privilege and challenge to write newspaper editorial and sports columns, and later magazine articles and poetry. Writing provided opportunities to express my opinions, analyses, insights and positions on just about anything. With that came a responsibility to the reading public I will never take lightly.

2: View from the Cave
If only these words would speak for all of mankind:
"I will fight no more forever."—Nez Perce Indian Chief Joseph, 1877.

3: Sandburg Homage
The poem and short biography are offered in heartfelt homage and with deep humility to the memory of Carl Sandburg (1878-1967). I first read Sandburg poetry many years ago and especially love The Fog. I have taken the liberty to use its format for a poetic paean to him.

Sandburg cherished his family and country, and honored all people through insightful and inspirational writings for more than 60 years. He flourished on his beloved farm within the Blue Ridge Mountains of western North Carolina, Connemara, where he contentedly spent the final 22 years of his fabled writing career and life.

Widely recognized as The People's Poet, Mr. Sandburg won a Pulitzer Prize in 1940 for "Abraham Lincoln: The War Years", a four-volume biography. Incredibly, he earned a second Pulitzer for "Complete Poems" in 1951 and received an International Poets Laureate Award. He was given the Presidential Medal of Freedom in

1963, and honors from the NAACP for lifetime efforts to broaden the frontiers of social justice. The great writer championed justice, especially for America's working people and children, through every possible venue: poetry, non-fiction, fiction, children's literature, magazines and folk-song minstrel.

I often contemplate the total Carl Sandburg as I meditate beside the still lake at Connemara in Flat Rock, in awe of his wordsmith ability, inspired by his humanity. I conjure him standing next to me beside the water or propped against a tree helping me think, write on a notepad, craft thoughts to later memorialize. I can almost see the white-haired old poet spryly climbing a steep path through rustling amber brush at day's end in search of the comfort of family, and to write at night sprawled on the giant rock in the back yard and in the stately white-columned great house that in 1968 became a National Historic Site, the only one that honors a poet.

On a personal level, I just love these 'unimportant except to me' coincidences: Mr. Sandburg moved to Flat Rock N.C. at the exact same age as me; was first a journalist, then a writer, then a poet (at the opposite end of the talent spectrums, I confess); and was father to three children. And my serendipitous new address in Hendersonville is Sandburg Terrace, of course.

4: Journey

Those who accept others regardless of their faith or lack thereof inspire me with their religious hearts.

"Our religion is not one of paint and feathers, it is a thing of the heart."—old Seneca Indian saying.

5: The Bully Boys Club

For Mathew Shepherd, the Columbine dead and the victims of bullies everywhere.

6: Venting the Flame

Some rights are tougher to witness being abused than others.

"We do not consecrate the flag by punishing its desecration."—US

Supreme Court Justice William Brennan, June 21, 1989.

7: Owls Have No Teeth
   They do? Okay, then I guess I'll have to change the title to A Dromedary Has One Hump.

8: If In Doubt Leave Them Out
   That is what I choose to do but I should not have to. The country that the pledge is to guarantees that.

9: Haiku, Too
   Posthumous sake toasts and bows to Masaoka Shiki, founder of modern haiku as an independent poetic form, and to Kawahigashi Hekigoto for expanding its scope and understanding.

10: The Last At-Bat
    For dads everywhere.

11: Clickety-Click
    Did ever a catchy tune constantly play in your head no matter how hard you tried to turn it off, or a poignant memory like this? For me, a train whistling through the night is particularly moving (no pun intended).

12: Soldier's Lament
    This civilian's poetic speculation of how some of our men and women in the military may feel about killing in the pre-emptive war of invasion in Iraq. It is offered with deep respect for all those brave warriors who serve and protect our great nation.
    I am sincerely appreciative of the awesome and selfless sacrifices of our fighting forces in Iraq and around the world. Thanks to them, our bedrock American freedoms can and will survive any onslaught, defeat any foe. To them I wish to be clear: I am wholeheartedly in support of you! I am not anti-war. I am anti-unjust-pre-emptive war.

13: The Butterfly

The Butterfly is dedicated to all the valiant young women out there who have shed their cocoons and stretched their wings to make themselves and the world a better place. One of my daughters provided me with inspiration for this poem but it salutes all four of them, and maybe your daughters, too, for being thoughtful, beautiful, loving and kind. To each of them: thank you all for the love and wonderful memories now and yet to be made.

14: Drops of Dew

The dying African woman with a baby I saw on television one night seared into my mind. This is my attempt to capture a bit of the essence of the mother suffering in the barren world of a refugee camp. I hope it does justice to her and helps to promote relief from all of us to the less fortunate.

These words are so little so late that I am ashamed. We should all be ashamed unless we have helped or are willing to help destitute people in Africa or wherever they may suffer. Posing and posturing doesn't cut it: we must each do something, and now! Thank you Bono, Bill Clinton and all caring and sharing Americans who make our nation proud.

Note: I wondered until the very moment of writing this what I can and should do. I can and will pledge a portion of my earnings from The Little Book of Message Poetry to a credible African hunger relief fund. Please search the Internet for credible relief organizations and support efforts to relieve hunger and disease in Africa and the world. If you wish to share your thoughts about this important subject e-mail me: jackprather1@bellsouth.net

15: Small g

The lower case g is not intended to offend any god/God; it is in response to constant dissing if those who think like me by religious extremists such as Jerry Falwell, Pat Robertson, Franklin Graham and other mass media preachers in bully pulpits. The TV anchor in the movie Network said it well: I'm mad as hell (small h) and I'm not going to take it anymore.

6: Reality and Other Illusions
What do we really know for certain? Is not the best option to allow new information in and new answers out, to continuously seek and accept truth as you find it? Is that not better than the alternatives?

17: 26
I hope I made order out of chaos but suspect it's the reverse. All language emanates from the 26 alphabet letters; they are all we have to communicate with except for body language and expressive eyes. Select them well.

18: •
To all who are afflicted: keep hope alive, stay alive, be better, get well!

19: Connections
This says it: "The leg bone connected to the knee bone, the knee bone..."— "Dem Bones, Dem Bones, Dem Dry Bones," James Weldon Johnson, circa 1920.

20: Immigrants are Us
We need to begin now to find solutions to illegal immigration issue. "Give me your tired, your poor, your huddled masses yearning to be free."— From the Statue of Liberty welcome tablet, 1811.

21: Tragedy in Brooklyn
Life goes on. So do memories.

22: Questions of Choice
Acceptance of and respect for a woman's right to choose is my choice. I don't think legislating personal morality can work or is wise.

23: Joey
Searching, searching, searching! We've all done it.

24: Treasures
If you ever lived in Brooklyn as an astonishing percent of Americans have then you know the magic.

25: Sticks and Stones
They won't break my bones or my spirit but they hurt a little a lot.

26: The Longest Moment
Sometimes it takes an extraordinarily poignant moment to get in touch with your own humanity.

27: Lies, Fibs and Other Truths
When the facts seem incontrovertible, when your eyes can see what's happening, when your instincts are keen, don't cave! Truth should not be crafted to fit any theory or agenda; it should be the other way around.
"The basis of all authority is the supremacy of fact over thought."—A.N. Whitehead in a Princeton University lecture on 'The Function of Reason', 1929.

28: Recipe
Are you gourmet?
"I dreamt I was a loaf of bread sitting on a shelf and I got so hungry that I began to eat myself."—Jean Prather Weiner, high school sophomore, 1960.

29: Lacy and Connor
The prosecutors in the Peterson case did their job and the result was painful but proper. If jury nullification had not freed O.J.: Marcia Clark, Chris Darden and the detectives would have been immortalized and the Dream Team vilified. If only!

30: The Six Senses

All six senses—yes six! I count feeling among them. And all are free except for the food and beverage we taste: how fortunate! We all should appreciate each sense each day.

31: A Scarlet H

There are plenty more H's to pass around. I hope I do not now or will ever deserve one.
"The hypocrisy of the nation must be exposed; its crimes must be denounced; the propriety of the nation must be startled; the conscience of the nation must be aroused."—Frederick Douglass, former slave, July 4, 1852

32: Power

Examine and re-evaluate your own power or lack thereof and interpret the whys, and how you use it. Once you understand the nature of personal power use it wisely and well.

33: A Half-Truth

I better avoid NRA conventions and a fella' named Wayne. At last count an average of 33,000 Americans annually are killed by guns, giving new meaning to the trite slogan guns don't kill people, people kill people. I offer this revision: guns don't kill people, people with guns kill people.

34: Cutting and Running

Please process current information on the war in Iraq to update your conclusions about this topic as our world is changing rapidly. I will too.

35: Dark

Let all who fear fear stand and cheer.

36: Eminent Domain

"You may not know it but your home is for sale." So wrote Timothy

Sandefur in the Washington Post, citing more than 10,000 state and city condemnations of homes and businesses from 1998-to-2003 to make way for private companies to expand.

What eminent domain might mean to your or your neighbor is not a common topic around the dinner table but maybe should be.

When eminent domain becomes absolute dominion not a single citizen
is safe from the insatiable greed of its government.—J.B. Williams, June 2005.

37: Green Irish Eyes
Love is the best message of all; lucky, lucky me.

38: Taxes Are Good
Nothing is more negatively viewed than the four-letters-minus-one word considered more a curse: tax. America would be barren without financing but a much happier nation if the money was effectively monitored and administered.

And if taxes weren't cut for the rich at the expense of everyone else there would be greater fairness.

39: Heat
Hooray for Al Gore!

40: A Butterfly for Camryn
Shirley Temple should be so sweet, Dakota Fanning so beautiful. I admit to no prejudice, only the power of observation.

41: Kill
Woe be to us if we become them. A better way: no parole ever, barren solitary confinement if a killer kills again in prison.

42: Thing
I abhor what 'Thing' says but defend her right to say it. The unnecessary hurt she causes with caustic and unkind slanders is beyond

shameful—but then again she has no shame. Real dignity emanated from the 9/11 widow who said Thing has the right to say whatever she wants (even the incredibly cruel and moronic comment that she enjoyed her husband's death). As a five-year old I know often says: 'That's unbewievable'.

43: Run Deer Run
This is an old prayer that should become a motto for hunter sportsmen who kill or wound and then track wild game for the dinner table:
"Deer, I am sorry to hurt you but the people are hungry."—Choctaw Indian hunting prayer.

44: Staying Healthy
Just because you can afford health insurance don't turn a cold heart to those who do not.

45: Make a List
This is my method of considering decisions and reaching conclusions.
"The function of reason is to promote the art of life."—A. N. Whitehead in a Princeton University lecture on 'The Function of Reason', 1929.

46: White and Black
Americans should consider adopting Americans first.
"Now is the time to lift our nation from the quicksand of racial injustice to the solid rock of brotherhood."—from Martin Luther King's "I Have A Dream" speech, 1963.

47: The Conversation
So, I'm an eavesdropper!

48: Two Worlds
Voting to oppose minimum wage hikes that would allow hard-

working individuals and families to escape poverty is perhaps the most devastating economic crime any elected official could commit.

Too many Americans who belong to expensive country clubs, travel extensively, own multiple homes, finance their children to top colleges and universities, and own major assets are the first to freeze minimum wage hikes that might help a child eat a healthful meal or receive needed health care because his/her parents can't earn enough to stay ahead of inflation, let alone escape poverty.

Minimum wage earners are increasingly devastated by rising prices of gas, homes, health care, and necessities ad infinitum. If you care in your heart, your mind and your religion for the working poor, speak up now and demand a fair minimum wage for workers!
"Poverty is the worst form of violence."—Mahatma Gandhi

49: Serendipity

A sign bearing that beautiful word has been displayed at our home for as long as Pam and I have been together, almost a quarter-century as of this writing. It describes our time together.

50: Itty Bitty Ditty

This ditty is a tongue-in-cheek thank you for reading this little book. Several other ditties reside in the round file and will stay there until a groundswell from my reading public demands to read them. I'll wait.

—The End—

Printed in the United States
144054LV00005B/3/A